JUNETEENTH

A Celebration of Freedom

JUNETEENTH honors the saga of
African people in the United States
from slave ship to freedom

CHARLES A. TAYLOR

with illustrations by Charles A. Taylor II

OPEN HAND
PUBLISHING, LLC

OPEN HAND PUBLISHING, LLC
Greensboro, North Carolina

Charles A. Taylor: Family photograph

Dedicated to the memory of my parents, Ollie and Inez

SPECIAL THANKS:
To our friends and family who helped us celebrate Juneteenth and posed for some of the illustrations used in this book.

ACKNOWLEDGMENT:
Elizabeth Johanna

RESEARCHERS:
Lisa Pfaff, Charles Taylor

OPEN HAND PUBLISHING, LLC
P. O. Box 20207
Greensboro, NC 27420
336-292-8585 / 336-292-8588 FAX
E-mail: openhnd1@bellsouth.net
www.openhand.com

Design and Production: Deb Figen
ART & DESIGN SERVICE, artdesign@jps.net

Library of Congress Cataloging-in-Publication Data

Taylor, Charles A. (Charles Andrew), 1950-
      Juneteenth: a celebration of freedom / by Charles A. Taylor ; with illustrations by Charles A. Taylor, II.
          p. cm.
      Includes bibliographical references.
      ISBN 0-940880-68-7 (alk. paper)
      1. Juneteenth--Juvenile literature. 2. Slaves--Emancipation--Texas--Juvenile literature.
I.Title.

E185.93.T4 T39 2002
394.263--dc21

2002022062
Rev.

FIRST EDITION

Printed in Korea
06 05 04 03 02   5 4 3 2 1

CONTENTS

1 What Is JUNETEENTH?

JUNETEENTH — June 19, 1865, is considered to be the date the last slaves in America were freed.

The Civil War had ended with the surrender of Confederate General Robert E. Lee to Union General Ulysses S. Grant at Appomattox, Virginia on April 9, 1865. Although the rumors of freedom were widespread even prior to this time, actual emancipation did not come to Texas until General Gordon Granger rode into Galveston and issued *General Orders No. 3* on June 19th. This was almost two and a half years after President Abraham Lincoln had signed the *Emancipation Proclamation*.

Didn't the *Emancipation Proclamation* free the enslaved?

President Lincoln issued the *Emancipation Proclamation* on September 2, 1862, notifying the states in rebellion against the Union that, if they did not cease their rebellion and return to the Union by January 1, 1863, he would declare their slaves forever free. The proclamation did not apply to those slaveholding states that had not rebelled against the Union. As a result, about 800,000 slaves were unaffected by the provisions of the proclamation.

The proclamation was ignored, of course, by those states that seceded from the Union. It would take a civil war to enforce the *Emancipation Proclamation*. And it would take the 13th Amendment to the U.S. Constitution to formally outlaw slavery in the United States.

When is JUNETEENTH celebrated?

Annually, on June 19, Juneteenth is celebrated in more than 200 cities in the United States. Juneteenth is now a state holiday in several states. Some cities sponsor week-long celebrations, culminating on June 19, while others hold shorter celebrations.

Why is JUNETEENTH celebrated?

It symbolizes the end of slavery. Juneteenth has come to symbolize for many African Americans what the Fourth of July symbolizes for all Americans —

Freedom!

Juneteenth serves as a historical milestone reminding Americans of the triumph of the human spirit over the cruelty of slavery. It honors those African American ancestors who survived the inhumane institution of bondage. It demonstrates pride in the marvelous legacy of endurance and perseverance they left us.

Why not just celebrate the Fourth of July like other Americans?

Blacks do celebrate the Fourth of July in honor of American Independence Day, but history reminds us that blacks were still enslaved when the United States obtained its independence.

Why were the slaves in Texas the last to know that they were free?

During the Civil War, Texas did not experience any significant incursions by Union forces. Although the Union army made several attempts to invade Texas, they were thwarted by Confederate troops. As a result, slavery in Texas continued to thrive.

In fact, because slavery in Texas experienced such a minor interruption in its operation, many slave owners from other slaveholding states brought their slaves to Texas to wait out the war. News of the emancipation was suppressed due to the overwhelming influence of the slave owners.

Why do we celebrate?

J
U
N
E
T
E
E
N
T
H

JUNETEENTH
represents the joy of freedom —
the chance for a new beginning.

Unless we expose the truth about
the African American slave experience,
Americans won't be truly free.

Never must we forget our ancestors' endurance
of one of the worst slave experiences
in human history.

Every American has benefitted from the wealth
blacks created through over 200 years of free labor.
Juneteenth allows us to acknowledge that debt.

To encourage every former slaveholding state
to follow Texas' example and make
Juneteenth a state holiday.

Every day in America, blacks are reminded of
the legacy of slavery. Juneteenth counters that
by reminding us of the promise of deliverance.

Even on the journey to discover who we are,
Juneteenth allows us to reflect on where we've been,
where we're at and where we're going as a people.

NEVER GIVE UP HOPE is the legacy of our enslaved ancestors.
This legacy produced black heroism during the Civil War
and helped launch the modern civil rights era.

To proclaim for all the world to hear:
Human rights must never again become
subservient to property rights.

History books have told only a small part
of the story; Juneteenth gives us a chance
to set the record straight.

Freedom is always worth celebrating!

2 From Slavery to Freedom in the United States

To understand the significance of Juneteenth, one must understand the unique slave experience that blacks endured in the United States.

Voyage Across the Ocean

Most blacks were brought to America in slave ships shackled in chains, stacked like sardines in the ships' hulls. Ships that were packed tightly provided less than eighteen inches between the ceiling and floor, not enough space in which to sit up. In the darkness beneath the deck, blacks were forced to lay in sickening stench filled with waste, disease, body lice and rodents for up to twelve weeks. Often the dead weren't removed for days, and the seawater turned the decomposing bodies soup-like, creating an unbelievably horrible and suffocating odor.

Describing what it was like to be in this "floating coffin," an ex-slave wrote:

> *"I was soon put down under the decks and there I received such a salutation in my nostrils as I had never experienced in my life so that, with the loathsomeness of the stench and crying together, I became so sick and low that I was not able to eat...I now wished for the last friend, death, to relieve me."*
>
> — Olaudah Equiano

Olaudah's experience was all too typical. The journey from Africa to America, for millions of Africans, turned out to be a death voyage. They cried out in different African tongues, but their prayers went unanswered. They never again saw their homeland, Africa. Their tears were met with the lash. For many, no doubt, hope died forever.

The slave ships almost always carried more Africans than the cramped space would allow, as it was expected that not everyone would survive the trip. Those who died en route were thrown to the sharks that followed. The Africans who survived the filth, fevers and contagions often paid a severe physical and emotional price. Their skin literally peeled away from lying naked for weeks in the wooden hull. Sores festered and led to lifelong health problems. Epidemics such as smallpox were common on the voyage.

Horrors of Slavery

The West Indies was the first stop for many slaves heading for America, not only to "season" them for the life of cruelty that awaited them in America, but also to bring them back to health to make them more saleable.

After the seasoning period, which essentially consisted of breaking the

slave's will, the slave was considered ready for servitude. The slave was introduced early to the whip and soon learned that obedience was his only right.

If anyone doubts the horrors of slavery, he or she should read the slave codes that were law in all slaveholding states. Skeptics should study the function of the "slave breakers," the slave patrollers and the slave catchers. Further, doubters should visit a historical museum to study how the auction block was used, feel the branding irons and chains and then read slave narratives to find out how often slaves were beaten and tortured.

Finally, she or he should read the Federal Fugitive Slave Law of 1850, in which escaping from these horrendous conditions was made illegal.

> *Must I dwell in slavery's night*
> *And all pleasure take its flight*
> *Far beyond my feeble sight*
> *Forever?*

> — George Horton
> *The Slave's Complaint*
> Poem by a Slave, 1829

The American slave system was especially harsh in its total stripping of African people's humanity. The system was enforced through an elaborate set of laws commonly known as "black codes" or "slave codes," which legally classified the slave as "property" and gave the slave owner life-and-death power over his property.

As "chattel," blacks were sold, bartered, rented, deeded, used as collateral and treated worse than farm animals. Their marriages held no legal standing, so their families were not recognized. Families could be broken up and sold at the whim of the slave owner. Children were routinely snatched from their mothers' arms and sold.

> *"At the auction, I've seen them sell a family. Maybe one man would buy the mammy, another buy the pappy, and another buy all the children or maybe just one, like that. I've seen them cry like they were at a funeral when they were parted. They had to drag them away."*
>
> — James Brown, ex-slave

Slavery was by its very nature a brutal and evil institution. While the slave could be sentenced to death for disobeying a slave code, the owner could administer all forms of punishment, including death, with little fear of retribution.

Minor infractions cost the slave a severe beating; those caught reading or writing were often put to death. Slaves who rebelled were turned over to a professional slave breaker, whose job was to transform the slave into a docile, obedient worker. Through mutilation, torture and every conceivable degradation, the slave was forced to comply. Slaves were hunted, raped, bred like animals and lynched without remorse.

Perhaps the words of the famous orator, Frederick Douglass, who had escaped slavery, say it best:

> *"We have worked without wages, we have lived without hope, wept without sympathy and bled without mercy..."*

Black Resistance

Despite the penalty of death, resistance to slavery was common, and took many forms. It ranged from spitting in the owner's soup to escape attempts, work slow-downs, arson, suicide and armed rebellion. Resistance by the enslaved was so frequent that it is difficult to understand how the myth of the happy slave or the loyal servant could have lasted so long. Of course, to recognize the fact of widespread resistance is to condemn the institution of slavery all the more. Slaves resisted their bondage in whatever ways they could, and they were ever aware of the constraints of their enslavement.

White Allies

The majority of whites in the North and South did not own slaves. By the 19th century, an anti-slavery movement had developed in the North. Many Quakers and other white abolitionists, such as William Lloyd Garrison, spoke out forcefully against slavery. They supported the more than fifty black anti-slavery groups formed by free blacks in the North.

One of the most successful examples of whites and blacks working together to resist slavery was the creation of the *underground railroad*. It operated from 1831 until the Civil War, and served as an escape route that began on southern plantations and ran through "free" states, depending on several thousand black and white "agents." These people heroically risked their prosperity and even their lives to help the slaves escape.

Although there were underground stations in Illinois, Indiana, Pennsylvania and elsewhere, Ohio was the center of underground railroad activity. The most famous agent, Harriet Tubman, commonly known as "Moses," herself an escaped slave, brought more than three hundred slaves to freedom.

Southern Secession

The active opposition to slavery by abolitionists contributed to a growing division between free states and slaveholding states. During the antebellum period the South did not sit still while the anti-slavery movement grew in the North. Southern states succeeded in getting a number of laws passed to protect slavery, including the gag rule that prohibited petitions against slavery from even being discussed in Congress.

The law that eventually led to a showdown, however, was the Fugitive Slave Law, passed in 1850. This law allowed

Rivers were a crucial part of the route on the Underground Railroad. By cover of night, thousands of slaves escaped to their freedom.

owners to capture and return runaway slaves even if they escaped to free states. It further required northerners to assist in this, under threat of stiff penalty. This infuriated abolitionists, and opposition to slavery grew even stronger. When abolitionist John Brown was martyred before his plan to free the slaves was fulfilled, the battle lines were drawn.

With the election of Abraham Lincoln, in 1860, southern slaveholding states formally withdrew from the Union. The nation stood on the brink of a civil war, and the question of slavery had to be resolved.

Civil War

Edmund Ruffin, an old man who had long been an outspoken advocate of slavery and southern secession, fired the first shots at Fort Sumter, South Carolina, in April 1861, launching the nation into what was to be a bloody and brutal four-year civil war.

At the outset, President Lincoln said the war was to preserve the Union and not to free the enslaved. In fact, during the first year of the war, slaves that escaped to Union forces were returned to Confederate troops. Fighting stopped. Confederate soldiers arrived at Union camps waving a white flag and were permitted to remove all slaves. This policy continued until General Benjamin Butler finally put a stop to it by declaring captured slaves contraband.

Union forces realized the war was being prolonged because the Confederacy was making use of its enslaved population of approximately four million people as support troops. Slaves were providing food and supplies, building fortresses and serving in a variety of other support roles, which freed southern white males to fight for the Confederate army.

Clearly this fact had an impact on Lincoln's decision to issue the *Emancipation Proclamation*.

Emancipation Movement

Anti-slavery sentiment grew stronger as the war got underway. Republicans in the Congress passed two Emancipation Acts in 1862 abolishing slavery in the District of Columbia (April 16, 1862) and in all territories of the United States (June 19, 1862). Other congressional action forbade Union soldiers to return runaway slaves. A second Confiscation Act of July 17, 1862, declared all slaves of rebel masters "forever free." All this occurred *before* Lincoln issued his proclamation.

In fact, President Lincoln was not even the first to issue an "emancipation proclamation." General John Fremont, with General David Hunter, issued an Emancipation Proclamation to free slaves in their military districts.

However, they were overruled by Lincoln himself, who feared that slaveholding Union states such as Missouri, Delaware, and Maryland might join the Confederacy.

Lincoln was eventually pressured politically and militarily into taking a stronger stand. As a result, on September 22, 1862, he submitted the *Emancipation Proclamation* to Congress. The proclamation took effect January 1, 1863. It was ignored in most slaveholding states though.

It would take the 13th Amendment to the U.S. Constitution to officially end slavery in America, and the 14th Amendment to grant blacks citizenship. While it did not free some 800,000 slaves in those slaveholding states still loyal to the Union, it sent a clear signal that the days of slavery in the United States were numbered. Lincoln became the first American President to ever denounce slavery.

Perhaps the *Emancipation Proclamation*'s greatest effect, however, was that it changed the intent of the war — it turned a war for union into a war for freedom. The *Emancipation Proclamation* opened the door for former slaves and free blacks to become actively involved in the Union's war effort. As a result, thousands of blacks worked as laborers, medics, cooks, spies and blacksmiths. According to official records, over 170,000 black soldiers saw combat in the war, including some 30,000 who served in the Union navy.

Despite being given less pay than white soldiers, receiving less food and facing unending racial discrimination, black soldiers fought heroically in a war for the liberation of their people. Some 37,000 blacks lost their lives in the Civil War. Their mortality rate was nearly 40% greater than for white troops. They fought and died for a freedom many never saw but which they believed correctly would be achieved with their sacrifice.

Lincoln with his cabinet at the first reading of the *Emancipation Proclamation*

E M A N C I P A T I O N

Whereas on the 22nd day of September, in the year of our Lord 1862, a proclamation was issued by the President of the United States, containing among other things, the following, to wit:

That on the first day of January, in the year of our Lord 1863, all persons held as slaves within any State or designated part of a State the people whereof shall then be in rebellion against the United States shall be then, henceforward, and forever free; and the executive government of the United States, including the military and naval authority thereof, will recognize and maintain the freedom of such persons and will do no act or acts to repress such persons, or any of them, in any efforts they may make for their actual freedom.

That the Executive will on the 1st day of January aforesaid, by proclamation, designate the States and parts of States, if any, which the people thereof, respectively, shall then be in rebellion against the United States; and the fact that any State or the people thereof shall on that day be in good faith represented in the Congress of the United States by members chosen thereto at elections wherein a majority of the qualified voters of such States shall have participated shall, in the absence of strong countervailing testimony, be deemed conclusive evidence that such State and the people thereof are not then in rebellion against the United States.

Now, therefore, I, Abraham Lincoln, President of the United States, by virtue of the power in me vested as Commander-in-Chief of the Army and Navy of the United States in time of actual armed rebellion against the authority and government of the United States, and as a fit and necessary war measure for suppressing said rebellion, do, on this 1st day of January, A.D. 1863, and in accordance with my purpose so to do, publicly proclaimed for the full period of one hundred days from the first day above mentioned, order and designate as the States and parts of States wherein the people thereof, respectively, are this day in rebellion against the United States the following, to wit:

P R O C L A M A T I O N

Arkansas, Texas, Louisiana (except the parishes of St. Bernard, Placquemines, Jefferson, St. John, St. Charles, St. James, Ascension, Assumption, Terre Bonne, Lafourche, St. Mary, St. Martin, and Orleans, including the city of New Orleans), Mississippi, Alabama, Florida, Georgia, South Carolina, North Carolina, and Virginia (except the forty-eight counties designated as West Virginia, and also the counties of Berkley, Accomac, Northampton, Elizabeth City, York, Princess Anne, and Norfolk, including the cities of Norfolk and Portsmouth), and which excepted parts are for the present left precisely as if this proclamation were not issued.

And by virtue of the power and for the purpose aforesaid, I do order and declare that all persons held as slaves within said designated States and parts of States are, and henceforward shall be free; and that the Executive Government of the United States, including the military and naval authorities thereof, will recognize and maintain the freedom of said persons.

And I hereby enjoin upon the people so declared to be free to abstain from all violence, unless in necessary self-defense. And I recommend to them in all cases when allowed, to labor faithfully for reasonable wages, and I further declare and make known that such persons of suitable condition will be received into the armed service of the United States, to garrison forts, positions, stations, and other places, and to man vessels of all sorts in said service.

And upon this act, sincerely believed to be an act of justice, warranted by the Constitution upon military necessity, I invoke the considerate judgment of mankind and the gracious favor of Almighty God.

In witness whereof, I have hereunto set my hand and caused the seal of the United States to be affixed. Done at the city of Washington, this first day of January, in the year of our Lord one thousand eight hundred and sixty-three, and of the Independence of the United States of America the eighty-seventh.

— ABRAHAM LINCOLN

3 Texas as a Slave State

Texan slaves were the last to be freed. Their plight provides insight into the entire institution of slavery.

The first Anglos who settled in what was to become the state of Texas brought enslaved blacks with them. Blacks, both free and enslaved, had lived in the region since the 16th century. Slaves cleared much of the agricultural land in east and central Texas and participated in the early lumber industry. By the 1850s the majority of cowboys in east Texas were enslaved blacks. However, the greatest growth of the enslaved population in Texas accompanied the rise in cotton cultivation in east and central Texas during the 1830s and again in the 1850s.

During these periods, the demand for slave labor was so great that smugglers illegally brought in newly-captured Africans through Cuba to supplement the large numbers of slaves being brought in from neighboring states. By 1860, nearly a third of Texas' total population was slaves. The census of 1860 listed only 355 free blacks and nearly 200,000 slaves.

The conditions under which the bondsmen lived and worked varied. However, the typical life of the slave was grim. Most slaves worked five and a half days a week, from "can't see" in the morning to "can't see" at night. They were poorly fed, clothed and housed, and they were subjected to beatings or worse at the owner's discretion. Enslaved blacks were treated like mules, sold through newspaper ads or in public auction yards. As girls reached puberty, they were forced to start producing children quickly, to replenish the slave ranks and the owners' profits.

While Texas experienced few organized slave rebellions, resistance to slavery was widespread and constant. Since the Mexican government opposed slavery, escapes into Mexico were common, especially from southwestern Texas. Mexico buttressed its opposition to slavery by refusing to sign an extradition treaty with the United States for the return of fugitive slaves. By 1855, more than 4,000 escapees had made their way to northern Mexico.

Slavery was strongly supported in antebellum Texas, however, primarily because slaveholders dominated economic life there. Slave labor produced 90% of the cotton — Texas' main cash crop. Through the wealth they derived from free slave labor, slave owners controlled the social and cultural milieu as well.

With this vise-like grip over the society, it's easy to understand why most white Texans, even though they did not themselves own slaves, defended slavery with every imaginable excuse. This was especially true of newspaper editors and ministers, many of whom encouraged Texan citizens to go to war in order to preserve slavery.

During the Civil War, few battles were fought in Texas. Federal troops did not penetrate the state's interior. As a result, slavery experienced only minor interruptions. The major disruption which did occur was due to the use by Confederate forces of impressed slave labor to build fortifications and supply other manpower needs.

As word circulated throughout the Confederacy that slavery in Texas was affected little by the war, slave owners from Louisiana, Arkansas and Missouri sent their slaves westward to Texas. It is estimated that more than 200,000 enslaved blacks were sent to Texas so the slaveholders could avoid the confiscation and liberation of their human property by the Union forces.

When Lincoln issued the *Emancipation Proclamation,* news of it was suppressed in Texas. Even if slaves were aware of the proclamation they chose not to act on that knowledge for fear of punishment — even death. Blacks remained at the mercy of increasingly hostile owners who were watching their slave empire crumble. The owners didn't want any part of a free black community; they feared a slave rebellion if news of the emancipation leaked out.

"King Cotton" was Texas' main cash crop during the antebellum period. It required a massive labor supply, so the slave population increased dramatically.

Years later, former slaves remembered the Civil War years as a time of increased beatings and hardship, with the harshest punishments given to those who spoke favorably about President Lincoln or the Union cause.

As the war continued and Confederate losses mounted, news of impending freedom couldn't be suppressed. In early 1865, word spread that Union forces would soon be in control of Texas.

General Orders No. 3

When Union General Gordon Granger arrived in Galveston with his troops, large throngs of enslaved blacks turned out to greet him. On June 19, 1865, he issued *General Orders Number 3*, announcing the emancipation of the slaves in Texas.

General Orders Number 3 began Texas Reconstruction, yet, sadly, Granger's proclamation showed more concern for order and stability than for the newly acquired rights of black people. Granger's Order encouraged the freedmen to sign labor contracts and remain with their old masters.

Gordon Granger was one of many Union generals who served exclusively in the West. On sick leave much of the time after the Civil War, he died in Santa Fe, New Mexico Territory, in 1876.

Official.

HEADQUARTERS DISTRICT OF TEXAS.
GALVESTON TEXAS, JUNE 19, 1865.
General Orders, No. 3.

The people are informed that, in accordance with a proclamation from the Executive of the United States, all slaves are free. This involves an absolute equality of personal rights and rights of property between former masters and slaves; and the connection heretofore existing between them, becomes that between employer and hired labor. The Freedmen are advised to remain at their present homes, and work for wages. They are informed that they will not be allowed to collect at military posts; and that they will not be supported in idleness either there or elsewhere.

By order of

Major-General Granger
F.W. Emery, Maj. & A. A. G.

(Signed,)

4 The Meaning of JUNETEENTH —FREEDOM

When blacks in Texas heard the news, they alternately sang, danced and prayed. There was much rejoicing and jubilation. Their lifelong prayers had finally been answered.

Many of the slaves left their masters immediately upon being freed, in search of family members, economic opportunities — or simply because they could. They left with nothing but the clothes on their backs and hope in their hearts. Oh, freedom!

> *"When my oldest brother heard we were free, he gave a whoop, ran, and jumped a high fence, and told mammy good-bye. Then he grabbed me up and hugged and kissed me and said, 'Brother is gone, don't expect you'll ever see me any more.' I don't know where he went, but I never did see him again."*
>
> — Susan Ross

Freedom meant far more than the right to travel freely. It meant the right to name one's self, and many freedmen gave themselves new names. County courthouses were overcrowded as blacks also applied for licenses to legalize their marriages. Emancipation allowed ex-slaves the right to assemble and openly worship as they saw fit. As a result, a number of social and community organizations were formed — many of which originated from the church.

Freedom implied that, for the first time, United States laws protected the rights of blacks. There was a run on educational primers as freed men and women sought the education that had for so long been denied them. The Bureau of Refugees, Freedmen and Abandoned Lands, commonly known as the Freedmen's Bureau, was founded by Congress in March 1865 to provide relief services for former slaves. Schools were established and joined churches as centers of the newly freed communities. The promise of emancipation gave freedmen optimism for the future; few realized slavery's bitter legacy was just beginning to unfold and that equality was to remain an elusive dream. Oh, freedom!

At the beginning of Reconstruction, the period immediately following the end of the Civil War, rumors were rampant that every freedman would be given forty acres and a mule. Ex-slaves petitioned for land and, with

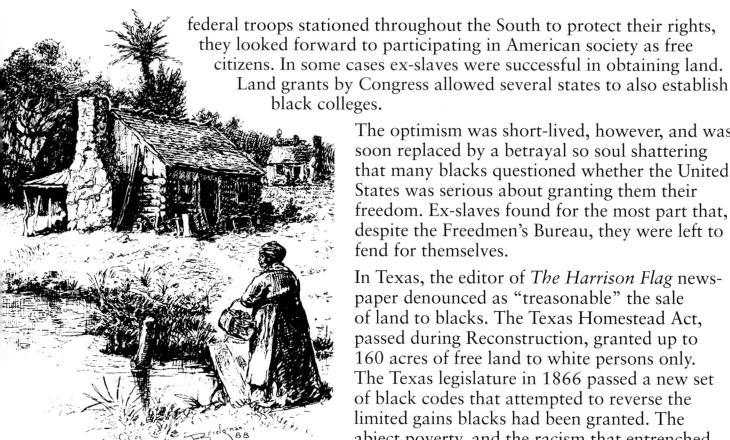

federal troops stationed throughout the South to protect their rights, they looked forward to participating in American society as free citizens. In some cases ex-slaves were successful in obtaining land. Land grants by Congress allowed several states to also establish black colleges.

The optimism was short-lived, however, and was soon replaced by a betrayal so soul shattering that many blacks questioned whether the United States was serious about granting them their freedom. Ex-slaves found for the most part that, despite the Freedmen's Bureau, they were left to fend for themselves.

In Texas, the editor of *The Harrison Flag* newspaper denounced as "treasonable" the sale of land to blacks. The Texas Homestead Act, passed during Reconstruction, granted up to 160 acres of free land to white persons only. The Texas legislature in 1866 passed a new set of black codes that attempted to reverse the limited gains blacks had been granted. The abject poverty, and the racism that entrenched it, along with the vested interests of the former slaveholders, suppressed any hope for assimilation into American society.

Ex-slaves entered freedom under the worst possible conditions. Most were turned loose penniless and homeless, with only the clothes on their backs. Ex-slaves were, as Frederick Douglass said, "free, without roofs to cover them, or bread to eat, or land to cultivate, and as a consequence died in such numbers as to awaken the hope of their enemies that they would soon disappear."

Many white Texans disdained black freedom. This utter contempt guaranteed the price of freedom for many would be unaffordable. The sharecropping system that emerged in Texas and all over the deep South kept many blacks from starving, but had little to distinguish it from the slave life blacks thought they had escaped. This was the other side of emancipation. High expectations gave way to heart-crushing disillusionment.

By 1877, the end of Reconstruction, the North , led by the emerging big businessmen created by war profits, abandoned black Americans to the will of the old southern slaveholding whites. Through Ku Klux Klan violence, racial discrimination and Jim Crow laws, they succeeded in disenfranchising the newly freed black people, resulting in an additional 100 years of oppression. It's not surprising that blacks turned to the only institution that gave them hope — the church.

5 The Black Church in Slavery and in Freedom

From the establishment of the first black church in America, throughout slavery and beyond, the church has been the foundation of the black community.

During the horrific days of slavery it provided relief and nourishment for the soul with its promise of a better life after death. The church gave the slave dignity and assured him he was equal in the eyes of God. Despite his earthly condition he was loved and valued as a child of God; no matter how difficult his burden became or unbearable his suffering was, Jesus, who too suffered, prepared a place of rest for him when his time was up on earth. It was this religious faith that sustained the slave and enabled him to endure his bondage.

The slave owner was able to observe a glimpse of this faith as he heard the incredible music that seemed to come out of the slave's soul while toiling in the field. If the slave owner had ventured into a slave church, his strong defense of slavery would no doubt have been weakened. He would have seen the people he considered inferior and sub-human without the defensive masks they wore in the fields. In their churches, enslaved men and women displayed a dignity and stateliness that survived the slave owner's dehumanizing oppression.

The church was more than a safe house. It served as a launching pad for black leadership and was involved early on in working for liberation. Many free blacks in northern churches participated in the Underground Railroad, raised money for freedmen after the Civil War, and helped keep the black community intact.

The importance of the black church cannot be overstated. It was, and perhaps still is, the single most important institution in the black community. It permitted self-expression and supported creativity at a time when such expression could have meant death. An example is found in the spirituals, gospel and other forms of music that helped blacks explain and endure their sojourn in America. Blacks were able to use their churches to hone organizational and leadership skills useful in the economic, social and political development of their community. It's no accident that Martin Luther King Jr., Jesse Jackson and a host of other civil rights leaders got their start through the black church.

Therefore it is not surprising that the black church has always played a pivotal role in keeping alive the meaning of Juneteenth. Religion has always been at the root of the observance of this holiday, which is ironic, considering it is a holiday born out of an institution so far removed from Christian ideals — slavery.

Traditional Prayer

The deep spiritual faith of the enslaved is reflected in the traditional prayer on page 21. Similar prayers are often recited in Juneteenth celebrations.

The Black Church provided a haven from the daily oppression faced by the slaves. After freedom, it also served as the center of social activities, including the sponsorship of the annual Juneteenth Celebration.

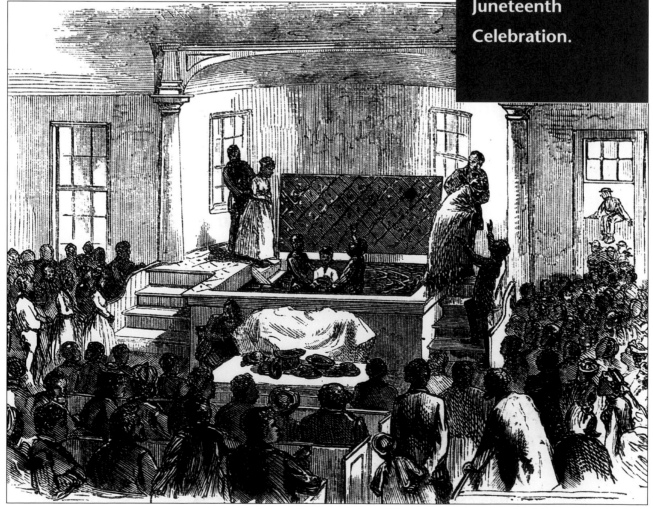

A Traditional Prayer

Father, I stretch my hand to thee — for no other help I know. Oh, my rose of Sharon, my shelter in the time of storm. My prince of peace, my hope in this harsh land. We bow before you this morning to thank you for watching over us and taking care of us. This morning you touched us and brought us out of the land of slumber, gave us another day — thank you Jesus.

We realize that many that talked as we now talked, this morning when their names were called, they failed to answer. Their voices were hushed up in death. Their souls had taken a flight and gone back to the God that gave it, but not so with us. We are thankful the sheet we covered with was not our winding sheet, and the bed we slept on was not our cooling board.

You spared us and gave us one more chance to pray. And Father, before we go further, we want to pause and thank you for forgiving our sins. Forgive all our wrong doings. We don't deserve it, but you lengthened out the prickly threads of our lives and gave us another chance to pray, and Lord for this we thank you.

Now Lord, when I've come to the end of my journey, when praying days are done and time for me shall be no more; when these knees have bowed for the last time, when I too, like all others must come in off the battlefield of life, when I'm through being 'buked and scorned, I pray for a home in glory.

When I come down to the river of Jordan, hold the river still and let your servant cross over during a calm down. Father, I'll be looking for that land where Job said the wicked would cease from troubling us and our weary souls would be at rest; over there where a thousand years is but a day in eternity, where I'll meet with loved ones and where I can sing praises to thee; and we can say with the saints of old, "Free at Last, Free at Last, thank God almighty, I am free at last."

Your servant's prayer for Christ sake. Amen!

— with additions from Reverend Wallace Evans

6 The Legacy of Slavery

The fact that it took a Civil War to forcibly put an end to slavery left a bitter legacy that continues to divide American society.

Slavery so bankrupted slave owners' sense of right and wrong that they were willing to die to defend that lifestyle. A slaveholding minority morally corrupted a nation, and this legacy still haunts the country.

According to historian John Hope Franklin, "the Founding Fathers [by allowing slavery] set the stage for every succeeding generation of Americans to apologize, compromise and temporize on those principles of liberty that were supposed to be the very foundation of our system of government and way of life...that is why this nation tolerated and indeed, nurtured the cultivation of racism that has been as insidious as it has been pervasive."

Professor Franklin asks, "How could the colonists make [such] distinctions in their revolutionary philosophy? They either meant that *all* men were created equal or they did not mean it at all. They either meant that *every* man was entitled to life, liberty, and the pursuit of happiness, or they did not mean it at all.... Patrick Henry, who had cried, 'Give me liberty or give me death', admitted that slavery was 'repugnant to humanity', but [obviously] not terribly repugnant, for he continued to hold blacks in bondage. So did George Washington and Thomas Jefferson...."

This blatant hypocrisy poisoned both religion and the law. Every institution at the slaveholder's disposal, including the church, was used to justify slavery and oppress black people. Instead of the slave owner being considered inhumane, the people he enslaved were. This legacy of racism must not be taken lightly. It has grown into perhaps the greatest internal threat that this country faces. John Hope Franklin put it aptly when he wrote that "slavery weakened America's moral authority."

It's amazing that, despite living under the most inhumane conditions known to humankind, blacks contributed to everything — from agricultural inventions to medical breakthroughs to music. Enslaved artisans crafted incredible sculptures, designed beautiful buildings and helped build a nation. We'll never know how many scientists, engineers, doctors and artists were lost on the trip over on the slave ships or after they arrived.

Despite all obstacles, blacks preserved a culture and succeeded in passing down a legacy of music, language, food, religion and a lesson in survival.

Slavery taught America another lesson, one that it too often ignores. Blacks and whites worked together to create an anti-slavery movement that ultimately succeeded. Later they fought and died together to force an end to slavery. Blacks and whites have worked throughout the nation's history for social justice. This lesson of cooperation must never be forgotten.

While the painful side of slavery makes it difficult for many blacks to celebrate Juneteenth, it is the positive legacy of perseverance and cooperation that makes it impossible for others to ignore.

JUNETEENTH honors the saga of African people in the United States from slave ship to freedom.

7 Juneteenth Celebrations Down Through the Years

Juneteenth is the oldest African American holiday observance in the United States.

Juneteenth became a legal holiday in Texas in 1980, largely due to the efforts of Texas State Representative Al Edwards. However, Juneteenth was widely celebrated by blacks in Texas long before that. In fact, it is the oldest African American holiday observance in the Unites States.

The celebration grew out of the euphoria surrounding the transition from slavery to freedom in Texas. Originally, it began as a day of talking, praying, storytelling and preaching. Freed men and women would use the day to give thanks, pass on oral traditions and plan the future. Celebrations began in Dallas as early as 1866, the very next year after the slaves in Texas were freed. Celebrants held religious services, competed in horse racing, enjoyed picnics and listened to fiddle and banjo playing.

By the late 19th and early 20th centuries the holiday was celebrated all over Texas and in neighboring states. Celebrations often included speeches by politicians, both black and white, and ended with a reading of the *Emancipation Proclamation.*

In several locations in Texas, permanent fairgrounds were established and became the sites of week-long celebrations centered on the Juneteenth anniversary. Churches planned the celebrations, but as Juneteenth grew in popularity, schools, Masonic lodges and other community-based organizations became sponsors. Today, more than thirty Texas cities celebrate the holiday annually. Houston hosts one of the largest celebrations in the state, featuring a wide range of educational, cultural and political activities.

While Juneteenth celebrations declined for a time during the height of the Civil Rights era, the holiday's revival during the past decade has been phenomenal. Juneteenth has spread beyond the borders of Texas, and today, it is a tradition — part of the cultural heritage of blacks — in more than 200 cities nationwide.

Milwaukee, Wisconsin, boasts one of the largest celebrations in the country, with more than 100,000 people attending. Other cities, such as Kansas City, Los Angeles and Houston draw huge crowds as well.

Comanche Crossing, near Mexia, Texas, was home to some of the largest Juneteenth celebrations in Texas. The celebration near Mexia dates back to 1889, and is among the oldest in Texas. Thousands of blacks made the annual pilgrimage to this site. Ex-slaves from Limestone County purchased the thirty-acre historic site in 1892 and named it Booker T. Washington Park, although the name never caught on. In the years before slavery, Comanche Indians crossed the river near the present site and the name "Comanche Crossing" is still used today.

Descendants built two major structures on the site: a dance pavilion that served both as a dance hall and food concession center, and a speaker's pavilion to hold commemoration services. Prior to the building of these two structures, Juneteenth programs were held under shade trees, tents or in the backs of horse-drawn wagons.

The focus is on building African American community pride through parades, fairs and performances. Many communities use the day to draw attention to a variety of political, cultural and economic initiatives. Like most African American holidays, many people celebrate Juneteenth both publicly and in the privacy of their homes.

Over the years, the celebration has evolved into four main components:

1) Mid-morning: PARADE

2) Noon: COMMEMORATION SERVICE

3) Afternoon: PICNIC & OUTDOOR RECREATIONAL ACTIVITIES

4) Evening: A DANCE

The speaker's pavilion at Booker T. Washington Park near Mexia, Texas

The holiday is known for its barbecues, baseball games, festivals, rodeos and parades. Church services and the singing of the Black National Anthem, "Lift Every Voice and Sing" by James Weldon Johnson, are annual traditions as well. Juneteenth has always been seen as a day of homecoming and family reunions. A big feast is often served mid-day, featuring an assortment of fried chicken, spare ribs, pork chops, greens of all sorts, black-eyed peas, home-made breads, cakes and pies. Homemade ice cream, red soda pop or Koolaid and watermelon have become closely associated with the holiday, too.

In many cities across the country, the Juneteenth parade has become a tradition. Elaborate floats, marching bands, celebrities and local politicians all add character and color to the day's festivities. Axes are often carried during the procession to depict the death of the slave owner. It is also customary to carry pine torches to symbolize the acquired freedom. Traditionally, ex-slaves always marched at the end of the procession and were greeted with respectful applause for surviving the horrors of slavery.

The pride of many an historic Juneteenth parade were the beautifully decorated buggies that competed for awards. Here Martha Yates Jones and Pinkie Yates sit in their buggy decorated for the 1908 Juneteenth parade. In the background is the Yates family home in Houston. Automobiles and floats are decorated now.

BLACK NATIONAL ANTHEM
Lift Every Voice and Sing

I.

Lift every voice and sing
Till earth and heaven ring,
Ring with the harmonies
   of Liberty;
Let our rejoicing rise
High as the listening skies,
Let it resound
   loud as the
   rolling sea.
Sing a song
   full of the faith
   that the dark past
   has taught us,
Sing a song
   full of the hope
   that the present
   has brought us,
Facing the rising sun
   of our new day begun
Let us march on
   till victory is won.

II.

Stony the road we trod,
Bitter the chastening rod,
Felt in the days
   when hope unborn
   had died;
Yet with a steady beat,
Have not our weary feet
Come to the place
   for which our fathers
   sighed?
We have come over a way
   that with tears has
   been watered,
We have come,
   treading our path
   through the blood
   of the slaughtered,
Out from the gloomy past,
Till now we stand at last
Where the white gleam of
   our bright star is cast.

III.

God of our weary years,
God of our silent tears,
Thou who has brought us
   thus far on the way;
Thou who has by Thy might
Led us into the light,
Keep us forever
   in the path, we pray.
Lest our feet stray
   from the places,
   Our God,
   where we met Thee,
Lest, our hearts
   drunk with the wine
   of the world,
   we forget Thee;
Shadowed beneath
   Thy hand,
May we forever stand.
True to our GOD,
True to our native land.

Lift Every Voice and Sing was written in 1901 by poet and civil rights leader James Weldon Johnson. The song's music was composed by his brother and songwriting partner, J. Rosamond Johnson. It was originally intended for use by Jacksonville, Florida schoolchildren in a program to celebrate the birthday of Abraham Lincoln. The song's popularity quickly spread throughout the African American communities of the South and became known as the "Negro National Anthem." Today, in the Black community, especially in programs of civil rights and other community organizations, *Lift Every Voice and Sing* still serves in this formal role, often being used to close the program on a "note" of spirited optimism.

Lift Every Voice and Sing by James Weldon Johnson, J. Rosamond Johnson
Used by permission of EDWARD B. MARKS MUSIC COMPANY

8 JUNETEENTH Today —

One Family's Celebration

Before the crack of dawn, Dad goes into the attic and gets the bell he keeps there just for Juneteenth. He rings it loudly, waking everyone up. As we stumble out of bed, we use only candlelight to find our way to the den. We get up early because Dad says that slaves started their day in the dark.

As the candlelight illuminates the wall chart of our family tree, Dad calls out each of the names of our ancestors who were enslaved — Willie, Emma, Tommy, Sarah, Ollie, Chicken John — until all the names have been called. After roll call, we close our eyes and imagine the slaves' lives — what the clothes were like, what the work was like and what food would be eaten each morning.

Mom leads us in the Black National Anthem, "Lift Every Voice and Sing." We bow our heads as Dad drops to his knees and prays the traditional prayer that many of our ancestors prayed. The prayer is so powerful that it always causes Mom to cry a little. We sing another song, usually a spiritual like "Go Down Moses."

Then we read the 13th and 14th Amendments to the Constitution of the United States. Some years we read the "Emancipation Proclamation," but Dad says it was these two Amendments that really freed blacks and made them citizens.

Before we are dismissed, Dad tells us to plan activities that symbolize freedom and that, after the family picnic and barbecue, we will present our activity.

Mom reaches into a shopping bag and gives us new clothes, which she says represent a new beginning. She tells us to wash away the old slave life as we bathe and, as we put on our new clothes, to step into freedom. Some years, instead of buying something new, we donate the money to the NAACP.

We make preparations for the picnic in our backyard. This is the fun part of Juneteenth, and it makes the day truly feel like a celebration. We decorate the yard and play outdoor games, we barbecue and just have a great time. We sing freedom songs and make homemade ice cream. Later in the afternoon, we sit down for a traditional Juneteenth dinner of barbecue, greens, freshly baked bread, pies, red soda, potato salad, home-made ice cream and watermelon.

Some years we celebrate Juneteenth in a neighborhood park with family and friends. We play softball, compete in foot races and listen to wonderful oral histories passed down from our ancestors. Everyone is asked to bring a dish to pass, made from an old family recipe. We savor the food and fellowship. As evening falls, our family continues the celebration at home.

We gather in the den to share our freedom activities. One year my brother Vashon planned a slave escape and gave us all roles to play. I played an agent on the Underground Railroad and I pretended to be Harriet Tubman's main contact in the state of Ohio. I made up code words and created secret hideaways for the slaves. As long as I was the agent, every enslaved person who passed through Ohio escaped to freedom.

This year Dad tells freedom stories that keep everybody on edge. Mom is planting a tree as her freedom activity, and she is putting up the memorial plaque I made in shop class to commemorate our ancestors. My cousin Lil performs a historical reading.

The years that Juneteenth falls on our family reunion, we rent a hall and share freedom activities with our extended family. Sometimes we watch parts of "Roots" and tell folktales, read slave narratives and sing freedom songs.

When it gets dark, we end the day the way we started. Dad rings the bell and we each light a candle. This time when Dad calls the roll, he calls our names as freedmen. We march outside and form a circle. It is so beautiful outside with the candles burning. We sing a freedom song softly and Dad tells a story of how our enslaved ancestors huddled like we are doing under the moonlight to plan their escape with nothing but their faith and the North Star to guide them.

We search the skies for the North Star and pause in silence when we locate it at the tail end of the Little Dipper. We pause for the thousands of our ancestors who used it to guide their way to freedom to the North. We pause because its brightness humbles us as we realize that a higher force in nature is at work — a force that led African Americans from bondage to freedom.

And as we gaze into the heavens, we remember all the world's peoples who were delivered from enslavement. We hope they rejoice in our freedom as we do theirs. We give thanks for freedom, and we dedicate ourselves to the tasks still to come, as the true meaning of Juneteenth sinks in.

Then we shoot off fireworks that light up the night sky, and in one loud voice salute our ancestors for their perseverance and their legacy. We pledge to never forget our past while keeping our eye on the future. After we say "FREE AT LAST, FREE AT LAST" in unison, we blow out the candles, bringing Juneteenth to an end.

GLOSSARY

Abolitionist • a person who worked to end both international slave trade and legal slavery in the United States.

Antebellum • the period prior to the American Civil War.

Black codes • also known as slave codes; a set of local, state and federal laws that protected the institution of slavery and controlled black lives; under these codes, blacks were stripped of all their human rights.

Chattel • moveable property; in the case of blacks, human beings who can be bought and sold as though they were moveable property.

Confederacy • the alliance of eleven southern slaveholding states that seceded from the United States in 1860–1861.

Contraband • items prohibited by law from being imported or exported; escaped slaves who made it to Union lines during the Civil War; such slaves could not be traded back to the Confederates, and hence were labeled "contraband."

Disenfranchisement • the systematic denial of a right of citizenship to an individual or group, such as the denial of the right to vote.

Emancipation • the process of freeing a person from forced servitude or slavery and restoring full legal rights.

Emancipation Proclamation • the proclamation issued by President Abraham Lincoln on January 1, 1863, freeing the enslaved in those territories still in rebellion against the Union.

14th Amendment • adopted July 28, 1868, officially granted blacks citizenship.

Freedmen's Bureau • (1865–1872), established during Reconstruction to act as a welfare agency for freed slaves in the South; although handicapped by inadequate funding and personnel, the bureau managed to build hospitals, schools and colleges for African Americans.

Fugitive Slave Law • a federal law enacted in 1850, which forced residents of free northern states to aid in the capture and return of runaway slaves to their owners.

Impressment • the forceful enlistment of people or property into public service, especially into military service during times of war.

Jim Crow • the system of laws which forced segregation of public facilities in southern states by race; enacted into law during the decade after the Civil War.

Lynching • execution by mob violence, especially the hanging of a person accused of a crime or social infraction without trial or legal authorization.

Patrollers • southern white males organized into regular patrols and authorized to enforce laws and rules restricting the movement of slaves.

Proclamation • an official public announcement.

Reconstruction • the post-Civil War period (1865–1877), during which the federal government attempted to rebuild, reunite and reconstruct the nation, especially the South; this period ended when federal troops were withdrawn from the South.

Seasoning • the process of breaking the slave's spirit into submission, to make an obedient slave; the systematic erosion of the slave's history, customs and traditions.

Secession • the withdrawal from the Union of the eleven southern slaveholding states in 1860–1861, which led to the Civil War.

Sharecropping • a system in which crops are produced in exchange for living on the land and "sharing the profit"; it became the legal mechanism by which blacks were kept in perpetual servitude, debt and control.

13th Amendment • adopted December 18, 1865; states "neither slavery nor involuntary servitude, except as a punishment for crime where-of the party shall have been duly convicted, shall exist within the United States, or any place subject to their jurisdiction."

Underground Railroad • a network of hiding places, safe houses and planned routes organized by abolitionists to help escaped slaves travel to their freedom either in northern states or Canada.

Union • the United States during the Civil War.

REFERENCES

Anyike, James C. *African American Holidays: A Historical Research and Resource Guide to Cultural Celebrations*. Chicago: Popular Truth Press, 1991.

Bankole, Katherine Kemi. *The Afrocentric Guide to Selected Black Studies Terms and Concepts*. Lido Beach: Whittier Publications, Inc., 1995.

Botkin, B.A., ed. *Lay My Burden Down: A Folk History of Slavery*. Chicago: University of Chicago Press, 1969.

Campbell, Randolph B. *An Empire for Slavery: The Peculiar Institution in Texas*. Louisiana State University Press, 1989.

Costello, Robert B. ed. *Random House Webster's College Dictionary*. New York: Random House, 1992.

Douglass, Frederick. *My Bondage and My Freedom*. New York: Arno Press and The New York Times, 1968.

Ebony Pictorial *History of Black America*. (Vol I) Nashville: Southwestern Company, 1971.

Editors of Time-Life Books. *Perseverance, African Americans Voices of Triumph*. Alexandria: Time-Life Books, 1993.

Edwards, Paul, abridged & ed. *Equiano's Travels: The Interesting Narrative of the Life of Olaudah Equiano or Gustavas Vassa,*

The African. Written by Himself, 1789. New York: Praeger, 1967.

Faust, Patricia L., ed. *Historical Times Illustrated Encyclopedia of the Civil War*. Carlisle: United States Army Military History, 1986.

Franklin, John Hope. "Slavery Left America with a Weak Moral Foundation," in *Slavery Opposing Viewpoints* by Dudley, William. Greenhaven Press, 1992.

Haley, Alex. *Roots*. Garden City: Doubleday & Company, Inc., 1976.

Harkavy, Michael D., ed. *The American Spectrum Encyclopedia*. New York: American Booksellers Association & Spectrum Database Publishing B.V., 1991.

Riley, Dorothy W. *My Soul Looks Back, 'Less I Forget*. New York: HarperCollins, 1993.

Smallwood, James M. *Time of Hope, Time of Despair: Black Texans during Reconstruction*. Kennikat Press, 1981.

Thomas, Karen M. "Texas Juneteenth Day." *Emerge Magazine* No. 4 Vol 8, p.31, June 30, 1993.

Tyler, Ronnie C. & Murphy, Lawrence R. *The Slave Narratives of Texas*. Austin: The Encino Press, 1974.

Wiggins, William H. *O Freedom!* Knoxville: The University of Tennessee Press, 1987.

Williams, David A. *Juneteenth: Unique Heritage*. Austin: Texan African-American Heritage Organization, Inc., 1992.

PHOTO CREDITS

[PAGE 4] "Colored troops, under General Wild, liberating slaves in North Carolina"; source: *Harper's Weekly*, January 23, 1864; credit: State Historical Society of Wisconsin, WHi (X3) 12575, CF 94584.

[PAGE 9] "Negroes Leaving Their Home"; source: *Harper's Weekly*, April 9, 1864 p. 237; credit: The Institute of Texan Cultures/University of Texas at San Antonio #73-1380.

[PAGE 11] "First Reading of the Emancipation Proclamation before the Cabinet"; Artist: A. H. Ritchie, 1866; Copyright owner: F.B. Carpenter; credit: Library of Congress LC-U5Z62-2070.

[PAGE 15] "Engraving of Negroes picking cotton" by Armand Welcker; source: Sweet, Alex E. & J. Amory Knox, *On a Mexican Mustang Through Texas*, London Chatoo & Windus, 1905, p.107; credit: The Institute of Texan Cultures/University of Texas at San Antonio #74-480.

[PAGE 16] "General Gordon Granger" by Matthew Brady; credit: National Archives 111-B-5624.

[PAGE 18] "On the old quarters"; source: Thompson, Maurice: *Story of Louisiana*. Boston: Lothrop, 1888 p. 289. credit: The Institute of Texan Cultures/University of Texas at San Antonio #75-29.

[PAGE 20] "Engraving of a Negro baptism in a church"; source: *Harper's Weekly*, June 27, 1874 p. 545; credit: The Institute of Texan Cultures/University of Texas at San Antonio #73-1604.

[PAGE 25] "Speaker's Pavilion, Booker T. Washington Park"; source: Texas Historical Commission; credit: Courtesy of the Texas Historical Commission, Austin TX.

[PAGE 26] "Martha Yates Jones and Pinkie Yates in a buggy decorated with flowers for 1908 Juneteenth Parade" by Schlueter; credit: Courtesy Houston Metropolitan Research Center, Houston Public Library, MSS 281–40.

RESOURCE ORGANIZATIONS

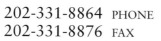

NATIONAL JUNETEENTH OBSERVANCE FOUNDATION (NJOF)
1100-15th St. NW
Suite #300
Washington, D.C 20005

202-331-8864 PHONE
202-331-8876 FAX

www.19thofJune.com
www.njof.org

Contact:
Reverend Ronald V. Myers, Sr., M.D.
Chairman

JUNETEENTH USA
P. O. Box 2910
Austin, TX 78768-2910

713-741-8800

Contact: Al Edwards

This organization seeks to educate people nationally and internationally about the cultural and spiritual significance of Juneteenth and advocates for the recognition of Juneteenth as a legal holiday by state legislatures.

ABOUT THE AUTHOR

Dr. Charles "Chuck" Taylor is the author and/or editor of eight books. He is currently the Assistant Dean for Graduate Programs at Edgewood College, a small private Catholic institution in Madison, Wisconsin. He has served as a national consultant to dozens of colleges and universities in the area of diversity and multicultural education. Chuck holds a master's degree in education from the University of Oregon, and a Ph.D. in Curriculum and Instruction from the University of Wisconsin–Madison.

He participates regularly in Juneteenth celebrations and believes passionately in the need to preserve African American cultural legacies. An educator for most of his professional career, Dr. Taylor has also been an entrepreneur, a documentary filmmaker, and a leader in promoting multicultural publishing. As a proud grandfather, Chuck strongly encourages families to keep the spirit of Juneteenth alive.

From the Publisher:

Open Hand Publishing, LLC is pleased that Charles Taylor has chosen us to produce this powerful and inspiring story. We publish *JUNETEENTH: A Celebration of Freedom,* with the hope that you, the reader, are moved to dedicate yourself to the ongoing struggle for freedom and human dignity.

Richard A. Koritz

OPEN HAND PUBLISHING, LLC